Motivation, Power & Goals

a daily journal

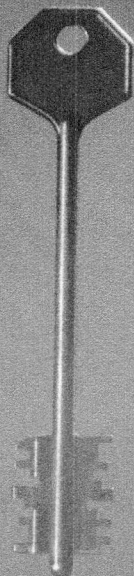

Written by Nancy Esfandiari & Greg Winston

Dedication

A special thanks to my amazing children Gianni,
and Nicole as well as my lovely sisters for their
continued support. Thank you, Greg my love of
life for motivating me to write.

Trust in yourself

> We need to stop
> looking to others for help.
> We need to begin to trust
> ourselves for guidance.
> With journaling,
> we draw out our own
> inner wisdom.

WinstonCommunications
CLARITY · COMPETENCE · COMMITMENT

www.GregWinston.com
unblockingyourpotential.blogspot.com

The art of journaling

The keeping of a personal journal has been a pursuit of a small percentage of the human society for hundreds of years. In the past men and women of learning, studiously kept a record of their days, their achievements and their dreams. I owe a great debt of gratitude to each one of them as I have learned so much and gained insight into my life.

For some people, the keeping of a journal is a natural extension of their everyday lives. How many of us have lifted the family Bible to discover small snippets cut from the newspaper, flowers pressed between the pages, envelopes with letters or pictures tucked away safely for future generations to discover? I certainly have found such treasures in the most 'ordinary' of books on the shelves of secondhand book shops and at garage sales. It always comes as a surprise and delight to discover them and then I feel a certain sadness that somehow these treasures have ended up in the hands of a stranger.

The unexpected gift of these objects has been a richer understanding of our desire to record and keep important memories and items and while tucking these treasures into the pages of a book isn't exactly journaling, it is a component of this amazingly creative and satisfying pass-time.

Journaling is a great way to process everything that you're going through, both high and low. Regularly keeping track of your emotions and the events of your life can serve as a barometer of your habits, strengths and tendencies.

Journaling Tools For Self-Empowerment
There's magic in journaling!

Journaling is one of the most powerful tools for self-growth.

Simple but effective, journaling can help you:

- Release pain, frustration and negative emotions like anger and fear
- Clear confusion and make good decisions more easily
- Grasp valuable insights that clear blocks and move you forward
- Spark your innate creativity
- Uncover and nurture a bigger picture for your life
- Reach new heights in self empowerment

Just writing down your thoughts is helpful. So imagine the potential when you intentionally focus the incredible powers of your conscious and subconscious minds… when you intentionally invite the quiet voice of intuition to speak through your writing.

Focused, Purposeful Journaling Tools Work Wonders!
Why is journaling so powerful?

Journal writing captures our thoughts and feelings on paper. This shows us how we think, create, learn and intuit. When we can see what we're thinking, we can work with our thoughts in new ways. We break through our habitual patterns to discover our innate wisdom and creative genius. And when we do this, our lives transform.

Journaling is a potent self-help tool even when used casually. And when we understand how it works, and use it by design, its power to heal and expand our abilities grows exponentially.

Helping You To Be Your Best!

We need to stop looking to others for help. We need to begin to trust ourselves for guidance. With journaling, we draw out our own inner wisdom.

I know the value of journaling for self-growth. To support you in being your best, I am offering you this quality journaling overview. Go deeper, reach higher… you'll never look back!

Journaling Instruction

Retreat to a secret, safe place where you can be alone with your thoughts. Make sure you're free from distraction and have a set time you can count on. This could simply be your bedroom with your phone off. I tend to write at the end of every day.

Review your day, write whatever comes to mind without self-editing. Many times things that are inside you and they just need to be expressed, and the journey of acknowledging all that helps to bring clarity and resolution. Decide that whatever you're thinking and feeling is ok because it's temporary.

Next, **write three good things** that happened today or three things that you caused to happen. Don't go deep and allow yourself to go off on tangents. Simply write "good" statements of facts ... all facts that are good.

Skip a line or two, then **write something you are grateful for.**

Last step... **write a goal for the next day.** This will give you the excitement of anticipation. With anticipation, your negative thoughts are buried or dismissed. At that moment you can begin your day with a positive force that's unequaled.

Keeping your journals and periodically refreshing your memory about your growth is a great source of encouragement as you face personal battles.

daily journal

by _____

_____

_____
date ended

daily journal

Aim to write something that comes straight from your stream of conciseness.

My Day · 3 Good Things · Grateful For · Goal For Tomorrow

_____

_____

_____

_____

_____

_____

_____

_____

_____

_____

_____

_____

_____

_____

_____

_____

_____

_____

_____

_____

_____

_____

_____

_____

_____

_____

daily *journal*

Aim to write something that comes straight from your stream of conciseness.

My Day · 3 Good Things · Grateful For · Goal For Tomorrow

_____

_____

_____

_____

_____

_____

_____

_____

_____

_____

_____

_____

_____

_____

_____

_____

_____

_____

_____

_____

_____

_____

_____

_____

_____

_____

daily *journal*

Aim to write something that comes straight from your stream of conciseness.

My Day · 3 Good Things · Grateful For · Goal For Tomorrow

_____

_____

_____

_____

_____

_____

_____

_____

_____

_____

_____

_____

_____

_____

_____

_____

_____

_____

_____

_____

_____

_____

_____

_____

_____

_____

_____

_____

daily journal

Aim to write something that comes straight from your stream of conciseness.

My Day · 3 Good Things · Grateful For · Goal For Tomorrow

_____

_____

_____

_____

_____

_____

_____

_____

_____

_____

_____

_____

_____

_____

_____

_____

_____

_____

_____

_____

_____

_____

_____

_____

_____

_____

_____

_____

daily journal

Aim to write something that comes straight from your stream of conciseness.

My Day · 3 Good Things · Grateful For · Goal For Tomorrow

daily *journal*

Aim to write something that comes straight from your stream of conciseness.

My Day · 3 Good Things · Grateful For · Goal For Tomorrow

_____

_____

_____

_____

_____

_____

_____

_____

_____

_____

_____

_____

_____

_____

_____

_____

_____

_____

_____

_____

_____

_____

_____

_____

_____

_____

_____

daily journal

Aim to write something that comes straight from your stream of conciseness.

My Day · 3 Good Things · Grateful For · Goal For Tomorrow

_____

_____

_____

_____

_____

_____

_____

_____

_____

_____

_____

_____

_____

_____

_____

_____

_____

_____

_____

_____

_____

_____

_____

_____

_____

_____

daily journal

Aim to write something that comes straight from your stream of conciseness.

My Day · 3 Good Things · Grateful For · Goal For Tomorrow

_____
_____
_____
_____
_____
_____
_____
_____
_____
_____
_____
_____
_____
_____
_____
_____
_____
_____
_____
_____
_____
_____
_____
_____

daily journal

Aim to write something that comes straight from your stream of conciseness.

My Day · 3 Good Things · Grateful For · Goal For Tomorrow

daily journal

Aim to write something that comes straight from your stream of conciseness.

My Day · 3 Good Things · Grateful For · Goal For Tomorrow

_____
_____
_____
_____
_____
_____
_____
_____
_____
_____
_____
_____
_____
_____
_____
_____
_____
_____
_____
_____
_____
_____
_____
_____
_____
_____
_____
_____

daily journal

Aim to write something that comes straight from your stream of conciseness.

My Day · 3 Good Things · Grateful For · Goal For Tomorrow

_____
_____
_____
_____
_____
_____
_____
_____
_____
_____
_____
_____
_____
_____
_____
_____
_____
_____
_____
_____
_____
_____
_____
_____
_____
_____
_____

daily journal

Aim to write something that comes straight from your stream of conciseness.

My Day · 3 Good Things · Grateful For · Goal For Tomorrow

_____

_____

_____

_____

_____

_____

_____

_____

_____

_____

_____

_____

_____

_____

_____

_____

_____

_____

_____

_____

_____

_____

_____

_____

daily journal

Aim to write something that comes straight from your stream of conciseness.

My Day · 3 Good Things · Grateful For · Goal For Tomorrow

_____

_____

_____

_____

_____

_____

_____

_____

_____

_____

_____

_____

_____

_____

_____

_____

_____

_____

_____

_____

_____

_____

_____

_____

_____

_____

_____

_____

daily journal

Aim to write something that comes straight from your stream of conciseness.

My Day · 3 Good Things · Grateful For · Goal For Tomorrow

_____

_____

_____

_____

_____

_____

_____

_____

_____

_____

_____

_____

_____

_____

_____

_____

_____

_____

_____

_____

_____

_____

_____

_____

_____

_____

daily journal

Aim to write something that comes straight from your stream of conciseness.

My Day · 3 Good Things · Grateful For · Goal For Tomorrow

_____

_____

_____

_____

_____

_____

_____

_____

_____

_____

_____

_____

_____

_____

_____

_____

_____

_____

_____

_____

_____

_____

_____

_____

_____

_____

daily journal

Aim to write something that comes straight from your stream of conciseness.

My Day · 3 Good Things · Grateful For · Goal For Tomorrow

_____

_____

_____

_____

_____

_____

_____

_____

_____

_____

_____

_____

_____

_____

_____

_____

_____

_____

_____

_____

_____

_____

_____

_____

_____

daily journal

Aim to write something that comes straight from your stream of conciseness.

My Day · 3 Good Things · Grateful For · Goal For Tomorrow

_____

_____

_____

_____

_____

_____

_____

_____

_____

_____

_____

_____

_____

_____

_____

_____

_____

_____

_____

_____

_____

_____

_____

_____

_____

_____

_____

daily journal

Aim to write something that comes straight from your stream of conciseness.

My Day · 3 Good Things · Grateful For · Goal For Tomorrow

daily journal

Aim to write something that comes straight from your stream of conciseness.

My Day · 3 Good Things · Grateful For · Goal For Tomorrow

_____

_____

_____

_____

_____

_____

_____

_____

_____

_____

_____

_____

_____

_____

_____

_____

_____

_____

_____

_____

_____

_____

_____

_____

_____

_____

daily journal

Aim to write something that comes straight from your stream of conciseness.

My Day · 3 Good Things · Grateful For · Goal For Tomorrow

_____
_____
_____
_____
_____
_____
_____
_____
_____
_____
_____
_____
_____
_____
_____
_____
_____
_____
_____
_____
_____
_____
_____
_____
_____
_____

daily journal

Aim to write something that comes straight from your stream of conciseness.

My Day · 3 Good Things · Grateful For · Goal For Tomorrow

_____
_____
_____
_____
_____
_____
_____
_____
_____
_____
_____
_____
_____
_____
_____
_____
_____
_____
_____
_____
_____
_____
_____
_____
_____
_____
_____
_____

daily journal

Aim to write something that comes straight from your stream of conciseness.

My Day · 3 Good Things · Grateful For · Goal For Tomorrow

daily journal

Aim to write something that comes straight from your stream of conciseness.

My Day · 3 Good Things · Grateful For · Goal For Tomorrow

_____
_____
_____
_____
_____
_____
_____
_____
_____
_____
_____
_____
_____
_____
_____
_____
_____
_____
_____
_____
_____
_____
_____
_____
_____
_____
_____

daily journal

Aim to write something that comes straight from your stream of conciseness.

My Day · 3 Good Things · Grateful For · Goal For Tomorrow

_____

_____

_____

_____

_____

_____

_____

_____

_____

_____

_____

_____

_____

_____

_____

_____

_____

_____

_____

_____

_____

_____

_____

_____

daily journal

Aim to write something that comes straight from your stream of conciseness.

My Day · 3 Good Things · Grateful For · Goal For Tomorrow

_____

_____

_____

_____

_____

_____

_____

_____

_____

_____

_____

_____

_____

_____

_____

_____

_____

_____

_____

_____

_____

_____

_____

_____

_____

daily journal

Aim to write something that comes straight from your stream of conciseness.

My Day · 3 Good Things · Grateful For · Goal For Tomorrow

_____

_____

_____

_____

_____

_____

_____

_____

_____

_____

_____

_____

_____

_____

_____

_____

_____

_____

_____

_____

_____

_____

_____

_____

_____

_____

_____

_____

daily journal

Aim to write something that comes straight from your stream of conciseness.

My Day · 3 Good Things · Grateful For · Goal For Tomorrow

_____

_____

_____

_____

_____

_____

_____

_____

_____

_____

_____

_____

_____

_____

_____

_____

_____

_____

_____

_____

_____

_____

_____

_____

_____

_____

_____

_____

daily journal

Aim to write something that comes straight from your stream of conciseness.

My Day · 3 Good Things · Grateful For · Goal For Tomorrow

_____
_____
_____
_____
_____
_____
_____
_____
_____
_____
_____
_____
_____
_____
_____
_____
_____
_____
_____
_____
_____
_____
_____
_____
_____
_____
_____
_____

daily journal

Aim to write something that comes straight from your stream of conciseness.

My Day · 3 Good Things · Grateful For · Goal For Tomorrow

_____

_____

_____

_____

_____

_____

_____

_____

_____

_____

_____

_____

_____

_____

_____

_____

_____

_____

_____

_____

_____

_____

_____

_____

_____

daily journal

Aim to write something that comes straight from your stream of conciseness.

My Day · 3 Good Things · Grateful For · Goal For Tomorrow

_____

_____

_____

_____

_____

_____

_____

_____

_____

_____

_____

_____

_____

_____

_____

_____

_____

_____

_____

_____

_____

_____

_____

_____

daily journal

Aim to write something that comes straight from your stream of conciseness.

My Day · 3 Good Things · Grateful For · Goal For Tomorrow

_____

_____

_____

_____

_____

_____

_____

_____

_____

_____

_____

_____

_____

_____

_____

_____

_____

_____

_____

_____

_____

_____

_____

_____

_____

Daily journal

Aim to write something that comes straight from your stream of conciseness.

My Day · 3 Good Things · Grateful For · Goal For Tomorrow

_____

_____

_____

_____

_____

_____

_____

_____

_____

_____

_____

_____

_____

_____

_____

_____

_____

_____

_____

_____

_____

_____

_____

_____

_____

_____

daily *journal*

Aim to write something that comes straight from your stream of conciseness.

My Day · 3 Good Things · Grateful For · Goal For Tomorrow

daily journal

Aim to write something that comes straight from your stream of conciseness.

My Day · 3 Good Things · Grateful For · Goal For Tomorrow

_____
_____
_____
_____
_____
_____
_____
_____
_____
_____
_____
_____
_____
_____
_____
_____
_____
_____
_____
_____
_____
_____
_____
_____
_____

daily journal

Aim to write something that comes straight from your stream of conciseness.

My Day · 3 Good Things · Grateful For · Goal For Tomorrow

_____

_____

_____

_____

_____

_____

_____

_____

_____

_____

_____

_____

_____

_____

_____

_____

_____

_____

_____

_____

_____

_____

_____

_____

_____

_____

_____

daily journal

Aim to write something that comes straight from your stream of conciseness.

My Day · 3 Good Things · Grateful For · Goal For Tomorrow

_____

_____

_____

_____

_____

_____

_____

_____

_____

_____

_____

_____

_____

_____

_____

_____

_____

_____

_____

_____

_____

_____

_____

daily journal

Aim to write something that comes straight from your stream of conciseness.

My Day · 3 Good Things · Grateful For · Goal For Tomorrow

_____

_____

_____

_____

_____

_____

_____

_____

_____

_____

_____

_____

_____

_____

_____

_____

_____

_____

_____

_____

_____

_____

_____

_____

_____

_____

daily journal

Aim to write something that comes straight from your stream of conciseness.

My Day · 3 Good Things · Grateful For · Goal For Tomorrow

_____
_____
_____
_____
_____
_____
_____
_____
_____
_____
_____
_____
_____
_____
_____
_____
_____
_____
_____
_____
_____
_____
_____
_____
_____
_____
_____
_____
_____

daily journal

Aim to write something that comes straight from your stream of conciseness.

My Day · 3 Good Things · Grateful For · Goal For Tomorrow

_____

_____

_____

_____

_____

_____

_____

_____

_____

_____

_____

_____

_____

_____

_____

_____

_____

_____

_____

_____

_____

_____

_____

_____

_____

_____

_____

_____

daily journal

Aim to write something that comes straight from your stream of conciseness.

My Day · 3 Good Things · Grateful For · Goal For Tomorrow

_____

_____

_____

_____

_____

_____

_____

_____

_____

_____

_____

_____

_____

_____

_____

_____

_____

_____

_____

_____

_____

_____

_____

_____

_____

daily journal

Aim to write something that comes straight from your stream of conciseness.

My Day · 3 Good Things · Grateful For · Goal For Tomorrow

_____
_____
_____
_____
_____
_____
_____
_____
_____
_____
_____
_____
_____
_____
_____
_____
_____
_____
_____
_____
_____
_____
_____
_____

daily.
journal

Aim to write something that comes straight from your stream of conciseness.

My Day · 3 Good Things · Grateful For · Goal For Tomorrow

daily journal

Aim to write something that comes straight from your stream of conciseness.

My Day · 3 Good Things · Grateful For · Goal For Tomorrow

_____

_____

_____

_____

_____

_____

_____

_____

_____

_____

_____

_____

_____

_____

_____

_____

_____

_____

_____

_____

_____

_____

_____

_____

_____

_____

daily journal

Aim to write something that comes straight from your stream of conciseness.

My Day · 3 Good Things · Grateful For · Goal For Tomorrow

daily journal

Aim to write something that comes straight from your stream of conciseness.

My Day · 3 Good Things · Grateful For · Goal For Tomorrow

_____
_____
_____
_____
_____
_____
_____
_____
_____
_____
_____
_____
_____
_____
_____
_____
_____
_____
_____
_____
_____
_____
_____
_____
_____
_____
_____

daily journal

Aim to write something that comes straight from your stream of conciseness.

My Day · 3 Good Things · Grateful For · Goal For Tomorrow

_____
_____
_____
_____
_____
_____
_____
_____
_____
_____
_____
_____
_____
_____
_____
_____
_____
_____
_____
_____
_____
_____
_____
_____
_____
_____
_____
_____

daily journal

Aim to write something that comes straight from your stream of conciseness.

My Day · 3 Good Things · Grateful For · Goal For Tomorrow

daily journal

Aim to write something that comes straight from your stream of conciseness.

My Day · 3 Good Things · Grateful For · Goal For Tomorrow

_____
_____
_____
_____
_____
_____
_____
_____
_____
_____
_____
_____
_____
_____
_____
_____
_____
_____
_____
_____
_____
_____
_____
_____
_____
_____
_____

daily journal

Aim to write something that comes straight from your stream of conciseness.

My Day · 3 Good Things · Grateful For · Goal For Tomorrow

_____

_____

_____

_____

_____

_____

_____

_____

_____

_____

_____

_____

_____

_____

_____

_____

_____

_____

_____

_____

_____

_____

_____

_____

_____

_____

_____

_____

_____

_____

daily *journal*

Aim to write something that comes straight from your stream of conciseness.

My Day · 3 Good Things · Grateful For · Goal For Tomorrow

_____

_____

_____

_____

_____

_____

_____

_____

_____

_____

_____

_____

_____

_____

_____

_____

_____

_____

_____

_____

_____

_____

_____

_____

_____

_____

daily journal

Aim to write something that comes straight from your stream of conciseness.

My Day · 3 Good Things · Grateful For · Goal For Tomorrow

_____
_____
_____
_____
_____
_____
_____
_____
_____
_____
_____
_____
_____
_____
_____
_____
_____
_____
_____
_____
_____
_____
_____
_____
_____
_____
_____

daily journal

Aim to write something that comes straight from your stream of conciseness.

My Day · 3 Good Things · Grateful For · Goal For Tomorrow

_____

_____

_____

_____

_____

_____

_____

_____

_____

_____

_____

_____

_____

_____

_____

_____

_____

_____

_____

_____

_____

_____

_____

_____

_____

daily journal

Aim to write something that comes straight from your stream of conciseness.

My Day · 3 Good Things · Grateful For · Goal For Tomorrow

daily journal

Aim to write something that comes straight from your stream of conciseness.

My Day · 3 Good Things · Grateful For · Goal For Tomorrow

_____

_____

_____

_____

_____

_____

_____

_____

_____

_____

_____

_____

_____

_____

_____

_____

_____

_____

_____

_____

_____

_____

_____

_____

_____

_____

_____

_____

daily journal

Aim to write something that comes straight from your stream of conciseness.

My Day · 3 Good Things · Grateful For · Goal For Tomorrow

daily journal

Aim to write something that comes straight from your stream of conciseness.

My Day · 3 Good Things · Grateful For · Goal For Tomorrow

daily journal

Aim to write something that comes straight from your stream of conciseness.

My Day · 3 Good Things · Grateful For · Goal For Tomorrow

_____

_____

_____

_____

_____

_____

_____

_____

_____

_____

_____

_____

_____

_____

_____

_____

_____

_____

_____

_____

_____

_____

_____

_____

_____

daily journal

Aim to write something that comes straight from your stream of conciseness.

My Day · 3 Good Things · Grateful For · Goal For Tomorrow

_____
_____
_____
_____
_____
_____
_____
_____
_____
_____
_____
_____
_____
_____
_____
_____
_____
_____
_____
_____
_____
_____
_____
_____
_____
_____

daily journal

Aim to write something that comes straight from your stream of conciseness.

My Day · 3 Good Things · Grateful For · Goal For Tomorrow

daily journal

Aim to write something that comes straight from your stream of conciseness.

My Day · 3 Good Things · Grateful For · Goal For Tomorrow

_____

_____

_____

_____

_____

_____

_____

_____

_____

_____

_____

_____

_____

_____

_____

_____

_____

_____

_____

_____

_____

_____

_____

_____

_____

_____

daily journal

Aim to write something that comes straight from your stream of conciseness.

My Day · 3 Good Things · Grateful For · Goal For Tomorrow

_____

_____

_____

_____

_____

_____

_____

_____

_____

_____

_____

_____

_____

_____

_____

_____

_____

_____

_____

_____

_____

_____

_____

_____

_____

_____

_____

daily journal

Aim to write something that comes straight from your stream of conciseness.

My Day · 3 Good Things · Grateful For · Goal For Tomorrow

_____

_____

_____

_____

_____

_____

_____

_____

_____

_____

_____

_____

_____

_____

_____

_____

_____

_____

_____

_____

_____

_____

_____

_____

daily journal

Aim to write something that comes straight from your stream of conciseness.

My Day · 3 Good Things · Grateful For · Goal For Tomorrow

daily journal

Aim to write something that comes straight from your stream of conciseness.

My Day · 3 Good Things · Grateful For · Goal For Tomorrow

_____
_____
_____
_____
_____
_____
_____
_____
_____
_____
_____
_____
_____
_____
_____
_____
_____
_____
_____
_____
_____
_____
_____
_____
_____
_____
_____
_____

daily journal

Aim to write something that comes straight from your stream of conciseness.

My Day · 3 Good Things · Grateful For · Goal For Tomorrow

_____

_____

_____

_____

_____

_____

_____

_____

_____

_____

_____

_____

_____

_____

_____

_____

_____

_____

_____

_____

_____

_____

_____

_____

daily journal

Aim to write something that comes straight from your stream of conciseness.

My Day · 3 Good Things · Grateful For · Goal For Tomorrow

daily *journal*

Aim to write something that comes straight from your stream of conciseness.

My Day · 3 Good Things · Grateful For · Goal For Tomorrow

_____

_____

_____

_____

_____

_____

_____

_____

_____

_____

_____

_____

_____

_____

_____

_____

_____

_____

_____

_____

_____

_____

_____

_____

_____

daily
journal

Aim to write something that comes straight from your stream of conciseness.

My Day · 3 Good Things · Grateful For · Goal For Tomorrow

daily journal

Aim to write something that comes straight from your stream of conciseness.

My Day · 3 Good Things · Grateful For · Goal For Tomorrow

daily journal

Aim to write something that comes straight from your stream of conciseness.

My Day · 3 Good Things · Grateful For · Goal For Tomorrow

daily *journal*

Aim to write something that comes straight from your stream of conciseness.

My Day · 3 Good Things · Grateful For · Goal For Tomorrow

daily journal

Aim to write something that comes straight from your stream of conciseness.

My Day · 3 Good Things · Grateful For · Goal For Tomorrow

daily journal

Aim to write something that comes straight from your stream of conciseness.

My Day · 3 Good Things · Grateful For · Goal For Tomorrow

_____

_____

_____

_____

_____

_____

_____

_____

_____

_____

_____

_____

_____

_____

_____

_____

_____

_____

_____

_____

_____

_____

_____

_____

_____

_____

_____

_____

_____

daily journal

Aim to write something that comes straight from your stream of conciseness.

My Day · 3 Good Things · Grateful For · Goal For Tomorrow

_____

_____

_____

_____

_____

_____

_____

_____

_____

_____

_____

_____

_____

_____

_____

_____

_____

_____

_____

_____

_____

_____

_____

_____

_____

daily journal

Aim to write something that comes straight from your stream of conciseness.

My Day · 3 Good Things · Grateful For · Goal For Tomorrow

daily journal

Aim to write something that comes straight from your stream of conciseness.

My Day · 3 Good Things · Grateful For · Goal For Tomorrow

_____

_____

_____

_____

_____

_____

_____

_____

_____

_____

_____

_____

_____

_____

_____

_____

_____

_____

_____

_____

_____

_____

_____

_____

_____

_____

daily journal

Aim to write something that comes straight from your stream of conciseness.

My Day · 3 Good Things · Grateful For · Goal For Tomorrow

daily journal

Aim to write something that comes straight from your stream of conciseness.

My Day · 3 Good Things · Grateful For · Goal For Tomorrow

daily journal

Aim to write something that comes straight from your stream of conciseness.

My Day · 3 Good Things · Grateful For · Goal For Tomorrow

_____
_____
_____
_____
_____
_____
_____
_____
_____
_____
_____
_____
_____
_____
_____
_____
_____
_____
_____
_____
_____
_____
_____
_____
_____
_____
_____

daily journal

Aim to write something that comes straight from your stream of conciseness.

My Day · 3 Good Things · Grateful For · Goal For Tomorrow

daily journal

Aim to write something that comes straight from your stream of conciseness.

My Day · 3 Good Things · Grateful For · Goal For Tomorrow

_____

_____

_____

_____

_____

_____

_____

_____

_____

_____

_____

_____

_____

_____

_____

_____

_____

_____

_____

_____

_____

_____

_____

_____

_____

_____

daily *journal*

Aim to write something that comes straight from your stream of conciseness.

My Day · 3 Good Things · Grateful For · Goal For Tomorrow

_____
_____
_____
_____
_____
_____
_____
_____
_____
_____
_____
_____
_____
_____
_____
_____
_____
_____
_____
_____
_____
_____
_____
_____
_____
_____
_____
_____
_____

daily journal

Aim to write something that comes straight from your stream of conciseness.

My Day · 3 Good Things · Grateful For · Goal For Tomorrow

_____

_____

_____

_____

_____

_____

_____

_____

_____

_____

_____

_____

_____

_____

_____

_____

_____

_____

_____

_____

_____

_____

_____

_____

_____

daily journal

Aim to write something that comes straight from your stream of conciseness.

My Day · 3 Good Things · Grateful For · Goal For Tomorrow

_____

_____

_____

_____

_____

_____

_____

_____

_____

_____

_____

_____

_____

_____

_____

_____

_____

_____

_____

_____

_____

_____

_____

_____

daily journal

Aim to write something that comes straight from your stream of conciseness.

My Day · 3 Good Things · Grateful For · Goal For Tomorrow

_____
_____
_____
_____
_____
_____
_____
_____
_____
_____
_____
_____
_____
_____
_____
_____
_____
_____
_____
_____
_____
_____
_____
_____
_____
_____
_____
_____
_____

daily journal

Aim to write something that comes straight from your stream of conciseness.

My Day · 3 Good Things · Grateful For · Goal For Tomorrow

_____

_____

_____

_____

_____

_____

_____

_____

_____

_____

_____

_____

_____

_____

_____

_____

_____

_____

_____

_____

_____

_____

_____

_____

_____

_____

_____

daily journal

Aim to write something that comes straight from your stream of conciseness.

My Day · 3 Good Things · Grateful For · Goal For Tomorrow

_____
_____
_____
_____
_____
_____
_____
_____
_____
_____
_____
_____
_____
_____
_____
_____
_____
_____
_____
_____
_____
_____
_____
_____
_____
_____

daily journal

Aim to write something that comes straight from your stream of conciseness.

My Day · 3 Good Things · Grateful For · Goal For Tomorrow

_____

_____

_____

_____

_____

_____

_____

_____

_____

_____

_____

_____

_____

_____

_____

_____

_____

_____

_____

_____

_____

_____

_____

_____

_____

_____

_____

daily journal

Aim to write something that comes straight from your stream of conciseness.

My Day · 3 Good Things · Grateful For · Goal For Tomorrow

_____

_____

_____

_____

_____

_____

_____

_____

_____

_____

_____

_____

_____

_____

_____

_____

_____

_____

_____

_____

_____

_____

_____

_____

_____

daily journal

Aim to write something that comes straight from your stream of conciseness.

My Day · 3 Good Things · Grateful For · Goal For Tomorrow

_____

_____

_____

_____

_____

_____

_____

_____

_____

_____

_____

_____

_____

_____

_____

_____

_____

_____

_____

_____

_____

_____

_____

_____

_____

_____

daily *journal*

Aim to write something that comes straight from your stream of conciseness.

My Day · 3 Good Things · Grateful For · Goal For Tomorrow

_____

_____

_____

_____

_____

_____

_____

_____

_____

_____

_____

_____

_____

_____

_____

_____

_____

_____

_____

_____

_____

_____

_____

_____

_____

_____

_____

_____

_____

_____

daily journal

Aim to write something that comes straight from your stream of conciseness.

My Day · 3 Good Things · Grateful For · Goal For Tomorrow

_____

_____

_____

_____

_____

_____

_____

_____

_____

_____

_____

_____

_____

_____

_____

_____

_____

_____

_____

_____

_____

_____

_____

_____

_____

_____

_____

daily *journal*

Aim to write something that comes straight from your stream of conciseness.

My Day · 3 Good Things · Grateful For · Goal For Tomorrow

daily journal

Aim to write something that comes straight from your stream of conciseness.

My Day · 3 Good Things · Grateful For · Goal For Tomorrow

_____

_____

_____

_____

_____

_____

_____

_____

_____

_____

_____

_____

_____

_____

_____

_____

_____

_____

_____

_____

_____

_____

_____

_____

_____

_____

_____

daily journal

Aim to write something that comes straight from your stream of conciseness.

My Day · 3 Good Things · Grateful For · Goal For Tomorrow

daily journal

Aim to write something that comes straight from your stream of conciseness.

My Day · 3 Good Things · Grateful For · Goal For Tomorrow

daily journal

Aim to write something that comes straight from your stream of conciseness.

My Day · 3 Good Things · Grateful For · Goal For Tomorrow

_____
_____
_____
_____
_____
_____
_____
_____
_____
_____
_____
_____
_____
_____
_____
_____
_____
_____
_____
_____
_____
_____
_____
_____
_____
_____

daily.
journal

Aim to write something that comes straight from your stream of conciseness.

My Day · 3 Good Things · Grateful For · Goal For Tomorrow

daily journal

Aim to write something that comes straight from your stream of conciseness.

My Day · 3 Good Things · Grateful For · Goal For Tomorrow

daily journal

Aim to write something that comes straight from your stream of conciseness.

My Day · 3 Good Things · Grateful For · Goal For Tomorrow

_____
_____
_____
_____
_____
_____
_____
_____
_____
_____
_____
_____
_____
_____
_____
_____
_____
_____
_____
_____
_____
_____
_____
_____
_____
_____

daily journal

Aim to write something that comes straight from your stream of conciseness.

My Day · 3 Good Things · Grateful For · Goal For Tomorrow

_____

_____

_____

_____

_____

_____

_____

_____

_____

_____

_____

_____

_____

_____

_____

_____

_____

_____

_____

_____

_____

_____

_____

_____

_____

_____

_____

daily journal

Aim to write something that comes straight from your stream of conciseness.

My Day · 3 Good Things · Grateful For · Goal For Tomorrow

_____
_____
_____
_____
_____
_____
_____
_____
_____
_____
_____
_____
_____
_____
_____
_____
_____
_____
_____
_____
_____
_____
_____
_____
_____

daily journal

Aim to write something that comes straight from your stream of conciseness.

My Day · 3 Good Things · Grateful For · Goal For Tomorrow

_____

_____

_____

_____

_____

_____

_____

_____

_____

_____

_____

_____

_____

_____

_____

_____

_____

_____

_____

_____

_____

_____

_____

_____

_____

daily journal

Aim to write something that comes straight from your stream of conciseness.

My Day · 3 Good Things · Grateful For · Goal For Tomorrow

_____
_____
_____
_____
_____
_____
_____
_____
_____
_____
_____
_____
_____
_____
_____
_____
_____
_____
_____
_____
_____
_____
_____
_____
_____
_____

daily journal

Aim to write something that comes straight from your stream of conciseness.

My Day · 3 Good Things · Grateful For · Goal For Tomorrow

_____
_____
_____
_____
_____
_____
_____
_____
_____
_____
_____
_____
_____
_____
_____
_____
_____
_____
_____
_____
_____
_____
_____
_____
_____
_____
_____
_____

daily journal

Aim to write something that comes straight from your stream of conciseness.

My Day · 3 Good Things · Grateful For · Goal For Tomorrow

_____

_____

_____

_____

_____

_____

_____

_____

_____

_____

_____

_____

_____

_____

_____

_____

_____

_____

_____

_____

_____

_____

_____

_____

_____

_____

daily journal

Aim to write something that comes straight from your stream of conciseness.

My Day · 3 Good Things · Grateful For · Goal For Tomorrow

_____
_____
_____
_____
_____
_____
_____
_____
_____
_____
_____
_____
_____
_____
_____
_____
_____
_____
_____
_____
_____
_____
_____
_____
_____

daily journal

Aim to write something that comes straight from your stream of conciseness.

My Day · 3 Good Things · Grateful For · Goal For Tomorrow

_____

_____

_____

_____

_____

_____

_____

_____

_____

_____

_____

_____

_____

_____

_____

_____

_____

_____

_____

_____

_____

_____

_____

_____

_____

_____

_____

_____

daily journal

Aim to write something that comes straight from your stream of conciseness.

My Day · 3 Good Things · Grateful For · Goal For Tomorrow

_____

_____

_____

_____

_____

_____

_____

_____

_____

_____

_____

_____

_____

_____

_____

_____

_____

_____

_____

_____

_____

_____

_____

_____

_____

daily journal

Aim to write something that comes straight from your stream of conciseness.

My Day · 3 Good Things · Grateful For · Goal For Tomorrow

_____

_____

_____

_____

_____

_____

_____

_____

_____

_____

_____

_____

_____

_____

_____

_____

_____

_____

_____

_____

_____

_____

_____

_____

_____

_____

_____

daily journal

Aim to write something that comes straight from your stream of conciseness.

My Day · 3 Good Things · Grateful For · Goal For Tomorrow

_____

_____

_____

_____

_____

_____

_____

_____

_____

_____

_____

_____

_____

_____

_____

_____

_____

_____

_____

_____

_____

_____

_____

_____

_____

_____

_____

_____

daily journal

Aim to write something that comes straight from your stream of conciseness.

My Day · 3 Good Things · Grateful For · Goal For Tomorrow

_____
_____
_____
_____
_____
_____
_____
_____
_____
_____
_____
_____
_____
_____
_____
_____
_____
_____
_____
_____
_____
_____
_____
_____
_____
_____
_____
_____
_____

daily journal

Aim to write something that comes straight from your stream of conciseness.

My Day · 3 Good Things · Grateful For · Goal For Tomorrow

_____

_____

_____

_____

_____

_____

_____

_____

_____

_____

_____

_____

_____

_____

_____

_____

_____

_____

_____

_____

_____

_____

_____

_____

_____

_____

daily journal

Aim to write something that comes straight from your stream of conciseness.

My Day · 3 Good Things · Grateful For · Goal For Tomorrow

daily journal

Aim to write something that comes straight from your stream of conciseness.

My Day · 3 Good Things · Grateful For · Goal For Tomorrow

_____

_____

_____

_____

_____

_____

_____

_____

_____

_____

_____

_____

_____

_____

_____

_____

_____

_____

_____

_____

_____

_____

_____

_____

_____

daily journal

Aim to write something that comes straight from your stream of conciseness.

My Day · 3 Good Things · Grateful For · Goal For Tomorrow

_____
_____
_____
_____
_____
_____
_____
_____
_____
_____
_____
_____
_____
_____
_____
_____
_____
_____
_____
_____
_____
_____
_____
_____
_____

daily journal

Aim to write something that comes straight from your stream of conciseness.

My Day · 3 Good Things · Grateful For · Goal For Tomorrow

daily journal

Aim to write something that comes straight from your stream of conciseness.

My Day · 3 Good Things · Grateful For · Goal For Tomorrow

_____

_____

_____

_____

_____

_____

_____

_____

_____

_____

_____

_____

_____

_____

_____

_____

_____

_____

_____

_____

_____

_____

_____

_____

_____

_____

_____

daily journal

Aim to write something that comes straight from your stream of conciseness.

My Day · 3 Good Things · Grateful For · Goal For Tomorrow

daily journal

Aim to write something that comes straight from your stream of conciseness.

My Day · 3 Good Things · Grateful For · Goal For Tomorrow

_____

_____

_____

_____

_____

_____

_____

_____

_____

_____

_____

_____

_____

_____

_____

_____

_____

_____

_____

_____

_____

_____

_____

_____

_____

_____

_____

_____

Daily journal

Aim to write something that comes straight from your stream of conciseness.

My Day · 3 Good Things · Grateful For · Goal For Tomorrow

_____
_____
_____
_____
_____
_____
_____
_____
_____
_____
_____
_____
_____
_____
_____
_____
_____
_____
_____
_____
_____
_____
_____
_____

daily journal

Aim to write something that comes straight from your stream of conciseness.

My Day · 3 Good Things · Grateful For · Goal For Tomorrow

_____
_____
_____
_____
_____
_____
_____
_____
_____
_____
_____
_____
_____
_____
_____
_____
_____
_____
_____
_____
_____
_____
_____
_____
_____
_____

daily journal

Aim to write something that comes straight from your stream of conciseness.

My Day · 3 Good Things · Grateful For · Goal For Tomorrow

_____

_____

_____

_____

_____

_____

_____

_____

_____

_____

_____

_____

_____

_____

_____

_____

_____

_____

_____

_____

_____

_____

_____

_____

_____

_____

daily journal

Aim to write something that comes straight from your stream of conciseness.

My Day · 3 Good Things · Grateful For · Goal For Tomorrow

_____

_____

_____

_____

_____

_____

_____

_____

_____

_____

_____

_____

_____

_____

_____

_____

_____

_____

_____

_____

_____

_____

_____

_____

_____

_____

daily journal

Aim to write something that comes straight from your stream of conciseness.

My Day · 3 Good Things · Grateful For · Goal For Tomorrow

_____

_____

_____

_____

_____

_____

_____

_____

_____

_____

_____

_____

_____

_____

_____

_____

_____

_____

_____

_____

_____

_____

_____

_____

_____

Daily journal

Aim to write something that comes straight from your stream of conciseness.

My Day · 3 Good Things · Grateful For · Goal For Tomorrow

_____

_____

_____

_____

_____

_____

_____

_____

_____

_____

_____

_____

_____

_____

_____

_____

_____

_____

_____

_____

_____

_____

_____

_____

_____

daily journal

Aim to write something that comes straight from your stream of conciseness.

My Day · 3 Good Things · Grateful For · Goal For Tomorrow

daily journal

Aim to write something that comes straight from your stream of conciseness.

My Day · 3 Good Things · Grateful For · Goal For Tomorrow

daily journal

Aim to write something that comes straight from your stream of conciseness.

My Day · 3 Good Things · Grateful For · Goal For Tomorrow

daily journal

Aim to write something that comes straight from your stream of conciseness.

My Day · 3 Good Things · Grateful For · Goal For Tomorrow

_____

_____

_____

_____

_____

_____

_____

_____

_____

_____

_____

_____

_____

_____

_____

_____

_____

_____

_____

_____

_____

_____

_____

_____

_____

daily journal

Aim to write something that comes straight from your stream of conciseness.

My Day · 3 Good Things · Grateful For · Goal For Tomorrow

daily journal

Aim to write something that comes straight from your stream of conciseness.

My Day · 3 Good Things · Grateful For · Goal For Tomorrow

_____

_____

_____

_____

_____

_____

_____

_____

_____

_____

_____

_____

_____

_____

_____

_____

_____

_____

_____

_____

_____

_____

_____

_____

_____

_____

daily journal

Aim to write something that comes straight from your stream of conciseness.

My Day · 3 Good Things · Grateful For · Goal For Tomorrow

_____

_____

_____

_____

_____

_____

_____

_____

_____

_____

_____

_____

_____

_____

_____

_____

_____

_____

_____

_____

_____

_____

_____

daily journal

Aim to write something that comes straight from your stream of conciseness.

My Day · 3 Good Things · Grateful For · Goal For Tomorrow

_____
_____
_____
_____
_____
_____
_____
_____
_____
_____
_____
_____
_____
_____
_____
_____
_____
_____
_____
_____
_____
_____
_____
_____
_____
_____

daily journal

Aim to write something that comes straight from your stream of conciseness.

My Day · 3 Good Things · Grateful For · Goal For Tomorrow

_____
_____
_____
_____
_____
_____
_____
_____
_____
_____
_____
_____
_____
_____
_____
_____
_____
_____
_____
_____
_____
_____
_____
_____
_____
_____
_____

daily journal

Aim to write something that comes straight from your stream of conciseness.

My Day · 3 Good Things · Grateful For · Goal For Tomorrow

_____
_____
_____
_____
_____
_____
_____
_____
_____
_____
_____
_____
_____
_____
_____
_____
_____
_____
_____
_____
_____
_____
_____
_____
_____
_____
_____
_____

daily journal

Aim to write something that comes straight from your stream of conciseness.

My Day · 3 Good Things · Grateful For · Goal For Tomorrow

daily journal

Aim to write something that comes straight from your stream of conciseness.

My Day · 3 Good Things · Grateful For · Goal For Tomorrow

_____

_____

_____

_____

_____

_____

_____

_____

_____

_____

_____

_____

_____

_____

_____

_____

_____

_____

_____

_____

_____

_____

_____

_____

_____

daily journal

Aim to write something that comes straight from your stream of conciseness.

My Day · 3 Good Things · Grateful For · Goal For Tomorrow

_____
_____
_____
_____
_____
_____
_____
_____
_____
_____
_____
_____
_____
_____
_____
_____
_____
_____
_____
_____
_____
_____
_____
_____
_____
_____

daily journal

Aim to write something that comes straight from your stream of conciseness.

My Day · 3 Good Things · Grateful For · Goal For Tomorrow

_____

_____

_____

_____

_____

_____

_____

_____

_____

_____

_____

_____

_____

_____

_____

_____

_____

_____

_____

_____

_____

_____

_____

_____

_____

_____

_____

_____

daily journal

Aim to write something that comes straight from your stream of conciseness.

My Day · 3 Good Things · Grateful For · Goal For Tomorrow

daily journal

Aim to write something that comes straight from your stream of conciseness.

My Day · 3 Good Things · Grateful For · Goal For Tomorrow

_____
_____
_____
_____
_____
_____
_____
_____
_____
_____
_____
_____
_____
_____
_____
_____
_____
_____
_____
_____
_____
_____
_____
_____
_____
_____
_____

daily journal

Aim to write something that comes straight from your stream of conciseness.

My Day · 3 Good Things · Grateful For · Goal For Tomorrow

_____

_____

_____

_____

_____

_____

_____

_____

_____

_____

_____

_____

_____

_____

_____

_____

_____

_____

_____

_____

_____

_____

_____

_____

_____

_____

daily journal

Aim to write something that comes straight from your stream of conciseness.

My Day · 3 Good Things · Grateful For · Goal For Tomorrow

_____

_____

_____

_____

_____

_____

_____

_____

_____

_____

_____

_____

_____

_____

_____

_____

_____

_____

_____

_____

_____

_____

_____

_____

_____

daily journal

Aim to write something that comes straight from your stream of conciseness.

My Day · 3 Good Things · Grateful For · Goal For Tomorrow

_____

_____

_____

_____

_____

_____

_____

_____

_____

_____

_____

_____

_____

_____

_____

_____

_____

_____

_____

_____

_____

_____

_____

_____

_____

daily journal

Aim to write something that comes straight from your stream of conciseness.

My Day · 3 Good Things · Grateful For · Goal For Tomorrow

_____
_____
_____
_____
_____
_____
_____
_____
_____
_____
_____
_____
_____
_____
_____
_____
_____
_____
_____
_____
_____
_____
_____
_____
_____
_____
_____

daily journal

Aim to write something that comes straight from your stream of conciseness.

My Day · 3 Good Things · Grateful For · Goal For Tomorrow

daily journal

Aim to write something that comes straight from your stream of conciseness.

My Day · 3 Good Things · Grateful For · Goal For Tomorrow

_____

_____

_____

_____

_____

_____

_____

_____

_____

_____

_____

_____

_____

_____

_____

_____

_____

_____

_____

_____

_____

_____

_____

_____

_____

_____

daily journal

Aim to write something that comes straight from your stream of conciseness.

My Day · 3 Good Things · Grateful For · Goal For Tomorrow

daily journal

Aim to write something that comes straight from your stream of conciseness.

My Day · 3 Good Things · Grateful For · Goal For Tomorrow

_____
_____
_____
_____
_____
_____
_____
_____
_____
_____
_____
_____
_____
_____
_____
_____
_____
_____
_____
_____
_____
_____
_____
_____
_____
_____
_____

daily journal

Aim to write something that comes straight from your stream of conciseness.

My Day · 3 Good Things · Grateful For · Goal For Tomorrow

daily journal

Aim to write something that comes straight from your stream of conciseness.

My Day · 3 Good Things · Grateful For · Goal For Tomorrow

daily journal

Aim to write something that comes straight from your stream of conciseness.

My Day · 3 Good Things · Grateful For · Goal For Tomorrow

_____

_____

_____

_____

_____

_____

_____

_____

_____

_____

_____

_____

_____

_____

_____

_____

_____

_____

_____

_____

_____

_____

_____

_____

_____

daily journal

Aim to write something that comes straight from your stream of conciseness.

My Day · 3 Good Things · Grateful For · Goal For Tomorrow

_____

_____

_____

_____

_____

_____

_____

_____

_____

_____

_____

_____

_____

_____

_____

_____

_____

_____

_____

_____

_____

_____

_____

_____

_____

_____

daily journal

Aim to write something that comes straight from your stream of conciseness.

My Day · 3 Good Things · Grateful For · Goal For Tomorrow

_____

_____

_____

_____

_____

_____

_____

_____

_____

_____

_____

_____

_____

_____

_____

_____

_____

_____

_____

_____

_____

_____

_____

_____

_____

_____

daily journal

Aim to write something that comes straight from your stream of conciseness.

My Day · 3 Good Things · Grateful For · Goal For Tomorrow

_____

_____

_____

_____

_____

_____

_____

_____

_____

_____

_____

_____

_____

_____

_____

_____

_____

_____

_____

_____

_____

_____

_____

_____

_____

_____

daily *journal*

Aim to write something that comes straight from your stream of conciseness.

My Day · 3 Good Things · Grateful For · Goal For Tomorrow

daily journal

Aim to write something that comes straight from your stream of conciseness.

My Day · 3 Good Things · Grateful For · Goal For Tomorrow

_____

_____

_____

_____

_____

_____

_____

_____

_____

_____

_____

_____

_____

_____

_____

_____

_____

_____

_____

_____

_____

_____

_____

_____

_____

daily journal

Aim to write something that comes straight from your stream of conciseness.

My Day · 3 Good Things · Grateful For · Goal For Tomorrow

_____

_____

_____

_____

_____

_____

_____

_____

_____

_____

_____

_____

_____

_____

_____

_____

_____

_____

_____

_____

_____

_____

_____

_____

_____

_____

_____

_____

daily journal

Aim to write something that comes straight from your stream of conciseness.

My Day · 3 Good Things · Grateful For · Goal For Tomorrow

daily.
journal

Aim to write something that comes straight from your stream of conciseness.

My Day · 3 Good Things · Grateful For · Goal For Tomorrow

Daily journal

Aim to write something that comes straight from your stream of conciseness.

My Day · 3 Good Things · Grateful For · Goal For Tomorrow

_____

_____

_____

_____

_____

_____

_____

_____

_____

_____

_____

_____

_____

_____

_____

_____

_____

_____

_____

_____

_____

_____

_____

_____

_____

_____

daily journal

Aim to write something that comes straight from your stream of conciseness.

My Day · 3 Good Things · Grateful For · Goal For Tomorrow

_____
_____
_____
_____
_____
_____
_____
_____
_____
_____
_____
_____
_____
_____
_____
_____
_____
_____
_____
_____
_____
_____
_____
_____
_____

daily journal

Aim to write something that comes straight from your stream of conciseness.

My Day · 3 Good Things · Grateful For · Goal For Tomorrow

daily journal

Aim to write something that comes straight from your stream of conciseness.

My Day · 3 Good Things · Grateful For · Goal For Tomorrow

_____
_____
_____
_____
_____
_____
_____
_____
_____
_____
_____
_____
_____
_____
_____
_____
_____
_____
_____
_____
_____
_____
_____
_____
_____
_____
_____
_____

daily journal

Aim to write something that comes straight from your stream of conciseness.

My Day · 3 Good Things · Grateful For · Goal For Tomorrow

daily journal

Aim to write something that comes straight from your stream of conciseness.

My Day · 3 Good Things · Grateful For · Goal For Tomorrow

daily journal

Aim to write something that comes straight from your stream of conciseness.

My Day · 3 Good Things · Grateful For · Goal For Tomorrow

_____
_____
_____
_____
_____
_____
_____
_____
_____
_____
_____
_____
_____
_____
_____
_____
_____
_____
_____
_____
_____
_____
_____
_____
_____

daily journal

Aim to write something that comes straight from your stream of conciseness.

My Day · 3 Good Things · Grateful For · Goal For Tomorrow

daily journal

Aim to write something that comes straight from your stream of conciseness.

My Day · 3 Good Things · Grateful For · Goal For Tomorrow

_____
_____
_____
_____
_____
_____
_____
_____
_____
_____
_____
_____
_____
_____
_____
_____
_____
_____
_____
_____
_____
_____
_____
_____
_____
_____
_____

daily journal

Aim to write something that comes straight from your stream of conciseness.

My Day · 3 Good Things · Grateful For · Goal For Tomorrow

_____
_____
_____
_____
_____
_____
_____
_____
_____
_____
_____
_____
_____
_____
_____
_____
_____
_____
_____
_____
_____
_____
_____
_____
_____
_____

daily journal

Aim to write something that comes straight from your stream of conciseness.

My Day · 3 Good Things · Grateful For · Goal For Tomorrow

daily journal

Aim to write something that comes straight from your stream of conciseness.

My Day · 3 Good Things · Grateful For · Goal For Tomorrow

_____
_____
_____
_____
_____
_____
_____
_____
_____
_____
_____
_____
_____
_____
_____
_____
_____
_____
_____
_____
_____
_____
_____
_____
_____

daily journal

Aim to write something that comes straight from your stream of conciseness.

My Day · 3 Good Things · Grateful For · Goal For Tomorrow

_____
_____
_____
_____
_____
_____
_____
_____
_____
_____
_____
_____
_____
_____
_____
_____
_____
_____
_____
_____
_____
_____
_____
_____
_____
_____
_____

daily journal

Aim to write something that comes straight from your stream of conciseness.

My Day · 3 Good Things · Grateful For · Goal For Tomorrow

_____

_____

_____

_____

_____

_____

_____

_____

_____

_____

_____

_____

_____

_____

_____

_____

_____

_____

_____

_____

_____

_____

_____

_____

_____

_____

_____

_____

Daily journal

Aim to write something that comes straight from your stream of conciseness.

My Day · 3 Good Things · Grateful For · Goal For Tomorrow

_____

_____

_____

_____

_____

_____

_____

_____

_____

_____

_____

_____

_____

_____

_____

_____

_____

_____

_____

_____

_____

_____

_____

_____

_____

_____

_____

_____

_____

daily journal

Aim to write something that comes straight from your stream of conciseness.

My Day · 3 Good Things · Grateful For · Goal For Tomorrow

_____

_____

_____

_____

_____

_____

_____

_____

_____

_____

_____

_____

_____

_____

_____

_____

_____

_____

_____

_____

_____

_____

_____

_____

_____

_____

_____

daily journal

Aim to write something that comes straight from your stream of conciseness.

My Day · 3 Good Things · Grateful For · Goal For Tomorrow

daily journal

Aim to write something that comes straight from your stream of conciseness.

My Day · 3 Good Things · Grateful For · Goal For Tomorrow

_____

_____

_____

_____

_____

_____

_____

_____

_____

_____

_____

_____

_____

_____

_____

_____

_____

_____

_____

_____

_____

_____

_____

_____

_____

daily journal

Aim to write something that comes straight from your stream of conciseness.

My Day · 3 Good Things · Grateful For · Goal For Tomorrow

_____

_____

_____

_____

_____

_____

_____

_____

_____

_____

_____

_____

_____

_____

_____

_____

_____

_____

_____

_____

_____

_____

_____

_____

daily journal

Aim to write something that comes straight from your stream of conciseness.

My Day · 3 Good Things · Grateful For · Goal For Tomorrow

_____

_____

_____

_____

_____

_____

_____

_____

_____

_____

_____

_____

_____

_____

_____

_____

_____

_____

_____

_____

_____

_____

_____

_____

_____

_____

_____

_____

Daily journal

Aim to write something that comes straight from your stream of conciseness.

My Day · 3 Good Things · Grateful For · Goal For Tomorrow

_____
_____
_____
_____
_____
_____
_____
_____
_____
_____
_____
_____
_____
_____
_____
_____
_____
_____
_____
_____
_____
_____
_____
_____
_____
_____

daily journal

Aim to write something that comes straight from your stream of conciseness.

My Day · 3 Good Things · Grateful For · Goal For Tomorrow

_____

_____

_____

_____

_____

_____

_____

_____

_____

_____

_____

_____

_____

_____

_____

_____

_____

_____

_____

_____

_____

_____

_____

_____

_____

Supercharging

Motivation to Supercharge Your Journaling

When you need additional push, or just a tiny bit of motivation . . . learn from those around us. Read the stories below, review the quotes a get inspired again. Now – go back to your journal and write to think deeper – write to create more impact. The goal of this section is to jump start you when you have writer's block. Let's go!

Attitude is Everything

The longer I live, the more I realize the impact of attitude on life.

Attitude is more important than facts.

It is more important than the past, than education, than money, than circumstances, than failures or successes, or what other people think or say or do.

It is more important than appearance, giftedness, or skill.

We can't change our past.

We can't change the fact that people will act in a certain way.

We have no control over the inevitable.

The only thing we can do is play on the one string we have, and that is our attitude.

The remarkable thing is we have a choice everyday regarding the attitude we will embrace for that day.

I am convinced that life is 10% what actually happens to me and 90% how I react to it.

And so it is with you.

- Charles R. Swindoll

Worrying Means You Suffer Twice

At the age of 45 most men are preparing for eventual retirement. However, "Zayah" a father of 5 young girls and a wife was interrupted by the protests and violence that started in his homeland of Iran. Because of his Christian beliefs in a largely Muslim country, he feared for the lives of his family. Rather than worry Zayah decided to do something about his fear.

In the dark of night, he moved quickly to put his wife and 5 children on a plane to America. Just as quickly he sold what few personal items he could. Leaving behind his home, rental property, trucks, and furnishings. He lost thousands of dollars and left Iran virtually penniless.

Armed with only a 3rd-grade education but a tremendous drive, Zayah joined his family in America. To prove his worth Zayah worked as a truck mechanic for one full day without pay. The owner was so impressed with his work Zayah was given a job. Within one year his drive and determination helped him to become a manager. He managed people who were born in America, who had an education and all of them were without his drive and unfading determination.

Years later he was directly responsible for growing the truck company that gave him a chance to start life in America. He purchased a 5-bedroom home for his family. He bought cars for his girls as they grew up. Later each of the daughters received down payments to buy homes as they married.

One could argue that Zayah's greatest gift to his family was that turbulence and bad times don't determine your life ... you do!

Always Have a Dream

Forget about the days when it's been cloudy,
but don't forget your hours in the sun...

Forget about the times you've been defeated,
but don't forget the victories you've won...

Forget about mistakes that you can't change now,
but don't forget the lessons that you've learned...

Forget about misfortunes you've encountered,
but don't forget the times your luck has turned...

Forget about the days when you've been lonely,
but don't forget the friendly smiles you've seen...

Forget about the plans that didn't seem to work
out right, but don't forget to always have a dream.

Going After What I Think About Most

At the tender age of 22, Gianni operates and a full-time student and full-time employee. His grades and in the top 5% of college students and his salary is currently at a middle-class status. Sounds good but it wasn't always good.

At his high school graduation, Gianni decided that high school would be enough for his future. His mother was very worried about his future and had a talk with Gianni about his future. She explained how his life would be without a college degree. That he would only have a minimum wage salary and never achieve the success he had dreamt of. Talks between Gianni and his mother continued. Gradually he began to see the value of changing his mind and continuing his education.

However, Gianni had a few things going that changed his life:

- He had a personality that attracted people and made them want to help him.

- He remained private and learned more about the people around him.

- He worked hard at each job he had and won promotions quickly.

- And the big one... Gianni dreamed of what he could have, what he could share and what was available to him to work on. Little by little his dreams became a reality. Whether it was a car or a job or a hobby he became what he thought about most. He accomplished what he thought about most. It's fascinating to me that in the era of "Gen-Xer's" this kid operates with what experts call an Old Soul. I'm Nancy and it's equally fascinating that he is my son.

The Balance

Every now and then in life we reach a point and we ask ourselves, "Is this where I want to be?

Why am I not happy? Will the depression pass?

Is my schedule wearing me out?

Is my relationship going in the right direction?

Is my career choice the right one?"

All these questions keep going through our minds trying to help us decide what changes to make.

The hard part is there are no right or wrong answers.

One person may be able to deal with the very same situations and be happy.

Other people may have made changes long ago.

We must remember that it is our decision based on how we feel.

Deep down there is this intuition that steers us in the right direction.

It is that little voice in the back of your mind that somehow knows what you need.

The only problem is that we don't always listen to it.

We often listen to the advice of others, who really don't know what makes you happy.

Life is so short.

We must strive to be happy.

Of course that does mean we must face unpleasant situations, but we need a balance to survive.

We must have good with the bad.

But once we lose that balance, we must restore it.

Little by little. Day by day.

We must keep positive and believe that one day we will smile again.

- I've learned that I should make the little decisions with my head and the big decisions with my heart. *– Age 52*

- I've learned that you can get by on charm for about fifteen minutes. After that, you'd better know something. *– Age 46*

- I've learned that you shouldn't expect life's very best if you're not giving it your very best. *– Age 51*

- I've learned that deciding whom you marry is the most important decision you'll ever make. *– Age 95*

- I've learned that you can't hug your kids too much. *– Age 54*

- I've learned that if you depend on others to make you happy, you'll be endlessly disappointed. *– Age 60*

- I've learned that children are the best teachers of creativity, persistence and unconditional love. *– Age 37*

- I've learned that if you wait until all conditions are perfect before you act, you'll never act. *– Age 51*

- I've learned that love will break your heart, but it's worth it. *– Age 26*

- I've learned that if love isn't taught in the home, it's difficult to learn it anywhere else. *– Age 51*

- I've learned that trust is the single most important factor in both personal and professional relationships. *– Age 20*

- I've learned that you shouldn't do anything that wouldn't make your mother proud. *– Age 51*

- I've learned that I still have a lot to learn. *– Age 92*

My Ancestors Sacrificed For Me to be Great

Anita is a product of a hardworking immigrant father. Her father was a hardworking, demanding strict disciplinarian who loved his family more than life itself. Because money was not plentiful early on, gifts were also not plentiful.

However, Anita received a gift that shaped her life and the lives of her siblings. The gift was a burning desire to dream a dream and to work hard and accomplish the dream.

Anita's dream was to own her own business. The early education she gained at the foot of her father along with her first jobs gave her greater motivation. Compiling lesson after lesson in small businesses Anita merged the training from her Dad with new strategies. Every day she came closer to her dream.

After years of working for others, Anita opened her own business - a luxury car rental company. Just as she began to enjoy the benefits of being an entrepreneur there was a tragic event. Her mentor, motivator and inspiration passed on ... her father died.

In the same way that her father had been the family patriot and anchor, Anita stepped proudly into the same role. She helped and supported her mother and four other siblings.

Anita's greatness was no accident. Her success was passed directly to her from a father who loved his family so much he gave them the gift of self-directed success.

Made in the USA
Coppell, TX
12 December 2020